PRAISING GOD: FAITH, HOPE AND LOVE

AF268768

Hope Williams

Copyright © 2022 by Hope Williams.

ISBN- 978-1-68506-061-9 (sc)

All rights reserved. No part of this book may be reproduced or transmitted in any form or by any means, electronic or mechanical, including photocopying, recording, or by any information storage and retrieval system, without permission in writing from the copyright owner.

The views expressed in this work are solely those of the author and do not necessarily reflect the views of the publisher, and the publisher hereby disclaims any responsibility for them.

InfusedMedia Co. LLC
www.infusedmedia.co
1-888-251-6088

TABLE OF CONTENTS

Praising God

Praising God is a collection of poetry based on the goodness of God, his blessings that I have received that have come through his son. It is for me a life-changing expression, from what was into what is supposed to be. It also gives meaning to the word **hope**, which is also my name.

What is it I want to tell the world, about me? Only that through all my trials, God has loved me and taught me to love Jesus as he does, except him as Lord and savior; and if I followed his instructions, there would be an abundance of love. And finally, to try to see the world through the eyes of Jesus and means that I had to develop the kind of faith that Hebrews 11:1 speaks about.

I won't be perfect, but I'll know that I can do all things through Christ who strengthens me daily. I thank my husband, Joe, my children, and friends because they are the ones who have helped in this learning process. I also want to thank my pastor and first lady, Rev. Charles and Jackie Lundy, for the sermons that have given me insight. But all praise, glory, and honor goes to God, Jesus, and the Holy Spirit because without them, there would be no words to write.

Hope

The Lights

The very time when the lights in my eyes should be shining toward God was when I found it hard to keep them on at all. Trouble would come, and I had not armed myself with the weapon God's word says we should put on in Ephesians 6:10. Without those weapons, my mind would roam.

A song came to mind, a song from years before when I was in the world. It said, "Turn out the lights, come closer," But Jesus was saying, "How can you not see that was is being sad in that song is exactly what you need to do with me? Come closer to me with the lights turned on, and tell the world what you now see. There is no problem I can't see, but you have to keep your mind stayed on me to find the relief you need."

It was so easy for me to blame people, places, and my circumstances for the things that made me so unhappy, but God expects more. I still thought I knew it all because I was always telling others what they should be thinking, feeling, and even doing with their life in their bad situations when I was the one who let my mind roam. What kind of Christian was I?

Doing What God Wants Now

To some, I might be growing old, but to God, I'm just becoming what he wants me to be. I used to think that what I was learning I should have already known. I now know that I wasn't ready for what I was about to discover. All of who I was to be was not in me so to speak. I mean that some of me needed to be repaired. Sounds like gibberish, but read on.

God is so amazing; I couldn't tell you enough just how wonderful he is. I thought about the eye contact that Jesus had with Peter, and then the conversation he had with him after the sacrifice. It took a little time before I saw the full picture because like Peter, I was in awe with the wonder of what Jesus could do more than the reason he was doing it. I had to read that particular part of John many times before I got the message. God already knew that Peter would be an eye-opening experience.

In many ways after that revelation I realized that surrendering all would also mean having it all. I just had to find out what having it all really meant. Now that I had a better understanding of what Jesus was saying to me, I also had to understand that Satan wasn't going to just quit messaging with me.

God wanted me to see some other things that were important to where he was taking me. There was going to be a day of assessment. The dictionary says that it is to decide fixed amount, value, or worth of something. I knew that the Lord was working hard to get me to see for myself what my quality of life should be. What I saw was the gift that I had been given that wasn't being used to its full potential.

I had so much to be thankful for, but what stood out above all else was God's patience. He watched as I kept doing the same things over and over, and he still waited for me to put my complete faith and trust in him above all else.

What I didn't have was focus. My concentration wasn't always on what was important. Pastor gave a message called Redeeming the Time. The best definition for the way things were with me was that I had to save myself from damnation or the consequences of sin, which meant I had to confess some things before I could be redeemed.

The message gave me a lot of insight on what I was about to see. God had given him one word that was a start of something different in my life. Total insight would come a little at a time because I had to go some places I'd never been before. I had to learn how to go through difficult situations in a completely different way. The new way would mean perseverance. I needed determination, I had to be committed, and I would have to follow through with important things until I finished them. Sharing with others all that are given to me by God.

My personal life overhaul, the assessment of my mind, which is a terrible thing to waste. Focus getting the lead out, the very thing that makes me slow to act. Perseverance, motivation to maybe inspire someone in the future not to waste as much time as I did. And then the legacy, what is it I want future generations to know. That they too can strive to be without spots or wrinkled and to express the gift that God has given them. To love God with the same passion that made him give his only son for our salvation. I gave to you God's gift to me.

Praise God

Praise God, all women and men,
Praise God, in him we do depend.
Satan will try with all his might,
To keep us from seeing
God's delivering light.
Praise God! Praise God! Praise God!
Praise God, who has all control,
Praise God, his word keeps us whole.
God is watching our every emotion,
To see how we share his word
In our daily devotion.
Praise God! Praise God! Praise God!
Praise God, he loves us so much,
Praise God, he's close
Enough to touch.
He'll close the gap between
Jesus and man,
And put his family back
Together again.
Praise God! Praise God! Praise God!

God's Plan For the Highest

Exhortation
For life's Trials and
Tribulations
Encouraging Souls of His
Creation
To Seek Jesus's Style of
Determination
Generalization Given to All
Situations
With Intensions Set on the
Heavenly Destination
…In Christ

First Feel His Feelings

I sat and thought about Jesus's life,

How his manner was always bright.

No matter what he was

going through,

He never let anyone

Change his mood.

I guess for a moment I felt ashamed,

That I sometimes asked blessings

In Jesus's name.

When there were times

When my attitude,

Showed little if any real gratitude.

He taught me to always live my life,

By God's Word, and I'd rise

To new heights.

All things are possible

The Bible does say,

But nothing will happen

If I cease to pray.

I know what is needed for me to do,

It's to feel his feelings, and

Share them with

You.

John 21:17,

He saith unto him the third

time Simon son of

Jonas, lovest thou me? Peter

was grieved because

He said to him the third

time, Do you love me?

And he said to him, Lord you

know all things, you

Know that I love you. Jesus

Saith Feed my Sheep.

The Passion of Christ What a Joyous Insight

I'm not the same person

I grew up to be,

Because of Christ's passion

and what I now see.

Jesus died on the cross,

I felt all his pain,

He asked my forgiveness,

he knew I was vain.

Always giving of his spirit

to those who are

lame

How in the world could I

ever be the same?

Because of his blessings

I have to renew,

My standing on issues I'm

no longer confused.

All things must be done

for the glory of God,

With feeling my actions

must come from my

heart.

How different my outlook

is on everyday life,

Remembering Jesus is my

personal sacrifice.

Act 1:8,

"But you will receive power when the Holy Spirit come on you; and you will be my witness in Jerusalem, and in Judea, and Samaria, and to the end of the Earth."

The Birth of Christ

What do we learn from

the birth of Christ?

That he's the missing ingredient

we need in our

life.

we've looked all over, chasing

after man,

When Jesus is always waiting,

to explain God's

Word to us again and again.

He said in God's Word, come and see,

If you want to find the true

meaning for my birth,

you must follow me.

Then go find your brother,

and tell him you have

found Christ,

He'll say what do you mean,

God already gave him

as our sacrifice.

But tell him there's so much

more to God's plan,

He wants us to follow closely,

he has stretched out

his hand

He said hold on tightly because

there's something

you should know,

That he loves us so much, we

don't ever have to let

go.

Matthew 11:29,

    Take my yoke upon you and learn from Me, for I am gentle and lowly in heart, and you will find rest for your souls.

A Mother's Love

A Mother's love is because

of God's grace,

Her mind he's prepared for

what she must face.

She'll jump for her babies

even when she's asleep,

God gives her the strength so

she'll land on her feet.

While giving her love, she'll

teach us to pray.

To fall on our knees and

Give Jesus the praise.

So if your mother is still on this earth,

Tell her you love her and

cause her no hurt.

The spirit she has is just

bursting with love,

A blessing that comes from

the Lord above.

John 19:26-27,

When Jesus saw his mother there and the discipline whom he loved standing nearby, he said to his mother; Woman, behold thy son! Then saith he to the disciple behold thy mother! And from that hour that disciple took her unto his home.

The Invitation

It was an invitation I
could not ignore,
I could be burden free
because of the Lord.
Did I hear what Jesus was
saying to me?
The weight of the world was
his, I had to believe.
And give him the things
that hurt me so much,
Even what's hidden way
down in my gut.
Because Jesus has already
prepared the way,
For me to say, "Yes! Yes!
Jesus I'll do what you
say."
And I'll keep on listening to
that still small voice,
That tells me daily I do have a choice.

1 Peter 5:6-7
    Therefore humble yourself under the mighty hand of God, that He may exalt you in due time, casting all your cares upon Him, for He cares for you.

Choice

God does absolutely nothing

for us by using any

force.

Deciding to receive Jesus

must completely be

our choice.

Boasting is our weakness;

It's what we do to host,

All who won't believe in

the promised Holy

Ghost.

Fragments of the Word of

God is all we've heard

at best,

And we've giving it our own

meaning and our

lives are just a mess.

Before accepting blessings

which are given

through the son,

The heart of man must be

prepared because of

where we are from.

The choice is always ours

each day to live a

righteous life,

Because nothing is impossible

when we are

doing what is right.

Then we'll see that God is

worthy of the praise

that is yet to come,

We have given him our

heartache, and we're no

longer feeling numb.

Joshua 24:15,

But if serving the Lord seems undesirable to you, then choose for yourself this day whom you will serve, whether the gods your forefathers served beyond the Rivers, or the god's of the Amorites, in whose land you are living. But as for me and my household, we will serve the Lord.

Gifts

The gifts God gives me I
had to discover,
They are there in his word
from cover to cover.
Always there in my deepest need,
Instruction given on how to retrieve,
The love of my father, which
I must be willing to
receive.
I examined my reason to
now trust in the Lord,
And I know the truth of the
matter is, he was who I
ignored.
I want you to know this
poem I now write,
It took some time because
my heart wasn't right.
I knew that my writing
meant the world to me,

It's my way to praise God for

being so good to me.

Corinthians 12:9,

And he said to me, My grace is sufficient for you, for my strength is made perfect in my weakness. Therefore I will boast the more gladly bout my weakness, so that Christ's power may rest on me.

The Seed

Seek the Lord and you will; find,

The joy God said would

be yours and mine.

God gave us his son, that he would be,

The seed on which we are to feed.

I'm telling you what I've

come to know,

God's Word was meant

to help us grow,

o in those times when

my life is a mess,

Because of the things I have

not yet confessed.

I'll give them to Jesus and I will see,

The life I lead will truly be free.

John 6:35,

 Then Jesus declared, I am the bread of life. He who comes to me will never go hungry, and he who believes in me will never be thirsty.

An Open Heart

The vocalist sang the song

with great power and

conviction,

She knew that through Jesus

an open heart would

never be an affliction.

To see the needs of others

more than ourselves,

And to know it's a feeling

that we have never felt.

God had already given us so

much through Jesus

Christ,

He endured much pain,

heartache, and strife.

But still his hearty was

open to everyone,

Sinful, self-righteous, or

whatever we had done.

To acknowledge God and to

do all things his way,

Jesus gave instructions for

why we should always

pray.

But still some things may

need to be rehearsed,

I don't think God will mind

because we'll learn that

He comes first.

Resist the devil and think of God,

Then cleanse your heart of

all things that set you

apart.

Open up your new heart

and let others in,

Jesus is the one who showed

us that with God we

always win.

John 3:16,
    "For God so loved the world that he gave His only begotten Son, that whosoever believes in Him shall not perish."

The Garments of God

Parents talk to their children
about almost
everything these days,
Some topics of discussion are
their clothes and what
they say.
Our appearance has been an
issue right from the
beginning,
Parents give their advice,
But their children just
aren't listening.
They disagree on what's
hot and what's not,
They think because we are
older we don't know a
whole lot.
Adam and Eve took a fig leaf
to cover what they
begin to see,
But their attempt at a cover
up was not meant to be.
Those two in the garden is
where this story began,

But their garment of salvation

was to come from an

animal's skin.

The story wasn't over they

had sinned and that's a

fact,

And the consequences would

continue from their

disobedient act.

Then Jesus came and taught

righteousness comes

from within,

God's word ways only through

Jesus is there

remission from all sins.

And the garments we wear

when self-respect has

been raised,

Say our eyes have been opened

and they give God

all the praise.

Genesis 3:21
    Unto Adam also and to his wife did the Lord God make coats of skins, and clothed them.

Self-Control

Think how different life
would be if we practiced
self-control,
Knowing that the things we
do don't have to be so
bold.
We are fighting with our
nei8ghbors when we don't
see eye to eye,
Both of us are cursing, and
we really don't know
why.
Then they see us showing
all the things that we
possess,
We know we've been taught
better but we're
dressing to impress.
Enticing the wrong influences,
and it's had a bad
effect,
And suddenly we realize that
we've lost all self-respect.
We have to be responsible for

the mistakes that we

have made,

When we've come to our

senses with Jesus as our

aide.

And now that we have decided

to practice self-control,

a new level of endurance

has got to be our goal.

Galatians 5:24,

Those who belong to Christ Jesus, have crucified the sinful nature with it's passion and desire.

God Bless the Children

Our children of today are in

need of correction.

They refuse to listen and follow

their parents'

direction.

They do everything in such a rush,

Sometimes it's hard to believe

they are a part of us.

Their friends give the orders

so they won't be bored,

They don't think it necessary

to trust in the Lord.

Our Purpose in life is to

give God the praise,

For the forgiveness he gives

the mistakes we have

made.

Our children don't realize

God knows all their

thoughts,

We remind them of Jesus,

their sins he has already

bought.

We want their lives to be filled

with love, hope, and

joy,

And a life the enemy won't

try to destroy.

God will open their eyes to

the supreme sacrifice,

And their spirits will proclaim

the promised eternal life.

1 John 3:1,

Behold! What manner of love the Father has bestowed on us that we should be called children of God! Therefore the, world does not know us, because it did not know Him.

The Mind

Where is my mind when
thoughts of others are
required?
How come I hear God but
I really don't abide?
What makes me think I've
passed life's most
important test?
When I'm much too busy to
see how much I've been
truly blessed.
And then I leave my church
because I really won't
agree.
With the way God's Word
said that it would be.
My heart is never faithful to
what I know is true,
I always end up doing the
things that Jesus would
never do.
And when it comes to loving
my neighbor as God's
Word has told me to,

My eyes are only focused on

the things I want from you.

I never stop to thank you Lord

for giving me your

best,

Your life you gave on Calvary,

so I'd want for

nothing less.

I want to say I'm grateful for

your love and how it's

grown,

Because I remember earlier

times when my feelings

were never shown.

2 Peter 1:2-3,

Grace and peace be multiplied to you in the knowledge of God and of Jesus our Lord, as his divine power has given to us all thing that pertains to life and to godliness through the knowledge of Him who called us by glory and virtue.

Commitments

I will follow you wherever
you go is what we've all
said,
But are we really ready for
what Jesus is offering as
our daily bread?
So I stopped and thought
about it for a minute,
Is this what I know as
being convenient?
As I gave what I said some
serious thought,
Jesus already knows my heart
the devil has caught.
Nothing Satan offers is worth
giving him any of my
time,
But he'll pray on my weakness
when I complain and
continue to whine.
The challenge is to defy the
wiles of the trickery
one,
Using the word of God, that

was given through his

son.

Then reflect on the mustard

seed as my example of

true faith,

It does more when grounded

and rooted, and on this

I should meditate.

My commitment will never be

the same,

God gave us all a gift that we

commit to in Jesus's

name.

Matthew 8:19,

Then a certain scribe came and said to Him, "Teacher I will follow you wherever you go."

Change

What is the change I have to except?
When life as I know it is
what I expected?
This is how my life has always been,
But I knew in my heart without
change I'd never
mend.
This old heart of mine could
stand as real change,
Because sometimes my
thoughts were really
deranged.
Jesus died on the cross so
that I would learn to
follow his lead.
And I was never to think
I knew all there is,
The pressures in life only
Jesus can ease.
I've only known Jesus for
such a short time,
Reality being I was still being primed.
Jesus is saying change comes
when you fight,

Life with his guidance, and

I'd stay in his sight.

God's change in my life

will really be nice,

He never does anything

that isn't precise.

Hebrews 4:16,
    Let us therefore come boldly to the throne of grace, that we may obtain
mercy and find grace to help in time of need.

Four Words

Assessing the quality of
my self-worth,
Because without purpose
how do I live on this
earth?
My purpose in life is what
I want to find,
But I have to be willing to
leave the past behind.
And preserve in my time of trouble,
What made me think I
wouldn't have to struggle?
And to the generation that
comes from the old,
What kind of legacy would
I want to be told?
Four words that have come to
mean the world to me,
Because some things in life
can still be received.

I am a part of God's flesh and bone,

That is what my focus

should only be on.

Psalm 121:1,
     I will lift up my eyes to the hills from whence comes my help.

My Hope

What an awesome name

to be given at birth,

Without really knowing its

meaning or worth.

I could hope for love, for

joy, and for peace,

I could hope for all the things

Jesus had preached.

But from time to time, I

would just sit and mope,

Because back then that was

how I would cope.

God gave me hope to be used

in my everyday living,

To teach me hope is better

than sinning.

It's expectation with

confidence in Jesus,

He is the only one who has

the power to free us.

But hope in our savior

come with a price,

That I too learn the meaning

of sacrifice.

Through kindness, goodness,

with patience in

faith,

Long-suffering and meekness,

is what it will take.

Hope is found in God's

fruit of the spirit,

They are all the things that

Jesus Exhibited.

Isiah 40:31,

But those who hope in the Lord, will renew their strength. They will soar on wings like eagles; they will run and not grow weary, they will walk and not faint.

God's Got My Back

Where is my faith when the

trouble of the world

comes?

And who do I thank for bringing

me from where I

started from?

God's blessing I just don't see,

I'm too busy looking for

his sympathy.

He'll heal my heartache and pain,

But most things in my life

will still remain the

same.

I'm just like the Israelite,

Thinking only of my own

personal plight.

All things in my life God's

got the facts,

But only through Jesus would

there be no more

lack.

I'm the one he wants to bless,

But the sin in my life I must confess.

Then when the trials of life begins,

I'll give them to Jesus and

stay free from sin.

He's watching the way that I react,

When I finally realize that

God's got my back.

Galatians 1:12,

For I neither received it from man, nor was I taught it, but it came through the revelation of Jesus Christ.

Bible Study

I'm studying the word of

God and I can see,

The knowledge I was lacking

has always been free.

As I open my Bible and wok

my way through,

I listen as Jesus explains

all that is true.

He wants more than ever

to give me new birth,

As if it were my first day

on this earth.

Then Jesus expresses

God's love for me,

And through God's Word, he

teaches how life should

really be.

I was thinking I had so

much time to play,

Just like they did back in Noah's day.

I'm studying the Bible the

knowledge is there,

It teaches there really is

a need for prayer.

Jesus's life on earth was

for a short time,

A more perfect example

will never be mine.

---

2 Timothy 3:16-17

All scripture is given by inspiration of God, and is profitable for doctrine, for instruction in righteousness, that the man of God may be complete, thoroughly equipped for every good work.

Experience the light

I'm going to do what I've never done,
I'm going to live a life of
victory, and it's really
going to be fun.
I'm going to see something
I've never seen,
While reading my Bible, I'll
find out what every
word means.
And celebrate the things
I see in the light,
Because I'll know I've given
the devil a real good
fight.
I've been just existing
for way too long,
Always cautions I'd say or
do something wrong.
But divine inspirational is given
when you trust in the
Lord,
Understanding his word
doesn't take too much
afford.

So with a pen or pencil in my hand,

And the image of God's promise land.

I'll be a vessel that he can use,

Because revelation of God's

Word is always good

news.

Isaiah 55:6,
    Seek the Lord while He may be found, call upon Him while He is near.

The Golden Leaves of Autumn

Open our eyes "oh Lord"

that we may see the

wonders of this earth,

The golden leaves of autumn,

when you give to

them new birth.

It's sad about their length of

days, but they too have

their reason,

And our seniors have the wisdom

to explain to us

the reason.

They see the beauty in the

trees and what it really

means,

The golden leaves of autumn

that used to be so

green.

So while you're looking at the

colors of the autumn

leaves,

You'll know that Jesus is

watching because you'll

feel his gentle breeze.

Job 12:12,
    Wisdom is with the aged men, And with length of days, understanding.

The Best Help

In a time when the world

is in such a mess,

One crisis after another is

what we are experiencing,

and we're living with less.

We feel as though we've been

thrown against a brick

wall,

Our patience has been shifted

away from the answer

to our urgent call.

Jesus who is supposed

to live within us,

But he has seen our reaction

to our problems, and

they just aren't good enough.

He expects us to be faithful

in our time of distress,

To never give up hope is not

too much to request.

God gave us Jesus, who taught

us how to get and

keep a grip,

He said love is the key that

would keep us

equipped.

With all the tools necessary

for the blessing we seek.

Because God's love, grace,

and mercy were not

designed to keep us weak.

Psalm 51:12,

    Restore to me the joy of your salvation and grant me a willing spirit, to sustain me.

Pure Motives

Pure motives is what my rock said,

I took the time to think,

is this what I had?

Pure was the word that didn't quite fit,

Transparent was I, God's

home run was just hit.

People are placed in our

everyday lives,

God uses them to teach us

we have not yet arrived.

Examination of self, I've

done once or twice,

But it's an everyday action

if not done I pay the

price.

What are my motives really made of?

Are they self-willed, or do

they come out of love?

Acts 5:1-4,

Now a man named Ananias, together with his wife Sapphira, also sold a piece of property. With his wife's full knowledge he kept back part of the money for himself, but brought the rest and put it at the apostles' feet.

Then Peter said Ananias, how is it that Satan has so filled your heart that you have lied to the holy Spirit and have kept for yourself some of the money you received for the land? Didn't it belong to you before it was sold? And after it was sold, wasn't the money at your disposal? What made you think of doing such a thing? You have not lied to men but to God.

The Fire Drill

How awesome is the Lord God above?
He showed us the building
is just a building He
supplied the love.
He took us that day onto
the parking lot,
I looked around the circle
and this is what I got.
Had we ever been this close before?
To examine our hearts, ask
forgiveness, and to
commune with the Lord.
This was our chance to
remember why we were
there,
As we looked up to heaven
and smelled God's fresh
air.
The gifts that God offers
could be carried out
anywhere.
With thanksgiving and love
now in our hearts,
The feelings that were revived

that gave our

salvation its start.

The new covenant says that

Jesus died once,

and it was for all,

And to commune together

is fulfillment to God's

heavenly call.

1 Corinthians 10:16-18,
    Is not the cup of thanksgiving for which we give thanks a participation in the blood of Christ? And is not the bread that we break a participation in the body of Christ? Because there is one loaf, we, who are many, are one body, for we all partake of the one loaf.

The Crowd

It doesn't matter if we are
alone or in a crowd,
We can shout we neeed Jesus
and not care if we're too
loud.
And say speak to us Lord,
we want to hear your
voice,
The world is trying to overrule
you, but they're just
making noise.
Jesus we'll cry, and he'll listen
to our need,
We need you to touch our
family, and revive their
unrooted seed.
No one gives us mercy like
us, it's all in God's
plan,
Because Jesus loves us more
than anyone else ever
can.
So when Jesus speaks everyone
has to pay attention,

Because if they don't, the

blessings that they're

seeking will never have recognition.

And they'll live life to the fullest after the seed has

started to grow,

The crowd has begun to shout

they need Jesus as

they see the blessings flow.

Mark 10:46-47

Then they came to Jericho. As Jesus and his disciples, together with a large crowd, were leaving the city, a blind man, Bartimaeus (that is, the Son of Timarus), was sitting by the roadside begging. When he heard that it was Jesus of Nazareth, he began to shout, Jesus Son of David, have mercy on me!

God's Greatest Gift

God's greatest gift. Take a minute and close your eyes and picture yourself hanging on the cross. Then image that all of what was done to Jesus is now being done to you. Now think about your reaction to what the people watching are saying to you. What are you screaming back at them before you take your last breath? Or are you as calm as Jesus who knew he had given us his very best while teaching us his father's will?

God had given us his greatest gift. He would become one of us, by living as we did with one very important exception. He would not let the flesh and all that Satan offered it tempt him into living as a sinner. God gave us Jesus. Then he gave us preachers, teachers, and other anointed people who would help in the life-changing process.

The messages from my pastor and the strong women who have come and gone in my life have been memorable. I've tried to get something from every sermon I've heard, but it wasn't always possible. I have even compared some of those messages to how the fruit of the Spirit works in our lives. Here are some examples. Love, a Gift from God, December 26, 1999. Joy, Seek the Lord First, January 4, 2004. Peace, Jesus will Work It out, July 29, 2001. Long-suffering, It's Time to Mind My Business, September 28, 2009. Gentleness Related to the spirit, June 4, 2000. Goodness, God Has Our Back, June 21, 2003. Meekness, In His Image, December 31, 2003. Faith, a Brand-New Day in Y2K, January 1, 2000. Temperance, Challenged By Christ, January 21, 2001.

There are so many sermons that have special meaning to me; they have come at a time when I needed the speaker to speak to me. I was in Bible study class a while back and the pastor who was teaching the class gave us an example of how we should live our lives. He told us about paradigm shift, a change in our basic assumptions. We have to learn how to be an example to others when it comes to the changes we make in our lives. And the group of women who were here for a while where I live that use to help those in need, because as they said they were, blessed to be a blessing, strong women of God whose example blessed me. I write this because sometimes that paradigm shift can go in the wrong direction, backward instead of forward, and some of my poetry may seems like a backward flip but I write what I'm shown through the spirit. Please read on, and may God bless you as he blessed me.

Selfishness or Me

Why do I think of myself more
highly than I ought?
Is it because of how I was
raised and the things I've
been taught?
Why is it that when someone
needs me I'm never
there?
And why doesn't it come natural
that I'm supposed to
share?
Or is this something new
that my spirit has never\felt?
The people closest to me are
who I refuse to please,
I think of them as the enemy,
even though I came
from the same seed.
Self-centered is my thinking,
it's deliberate act,
If I were to consider another's
feelings, it might get
the devil off my back.
The Bible says many who are

first will be last, and

the last first,

But If I leave Jesus out of

my life, it'll only get

worst.

2 Corinthians 8:9,

For you know the grace of our Lord Jesus Christ, that though He was rich, yet for your sakes He became poor, that you through His poverty might become rich.

Siblings Rivalry

My mom had eight children, three boys and five girls,

To some it was too many, but she brought us all into this world.

Our life wasn't always easy because we liked to fight and brawl,

Even though she taught us better, we let the devil make the call.

There were times we sat and watched as she shed so many tears,

Because we would not listen as she taught us throughout the years.

My siblings and I didn't get to say good-bye,

None of us were with her when the Lord closed her eyes.

Then things got much better with my siblings and I,

We had learned to love each other after giving it a try.

But now it's back to usual with my siblings and I,

Because of our refusal to let Jesus in on why.

Genesis 13:8,

So Abram said to Lot, "Please let there be no strife between you and me, and between my herdsmen; for we are brethren.

Hell's Pathway

Impostor's illustration of what life is supposed to be,

Aligning their conduct with demonic prophecy.

Every day there's destruction of God's word.,

Defining its content in ways that have never been heard.

Disaster is on our doorstep, but it's like we all are blind,

Disobedience and corruption is all that's on our minds.

We are executing judgement, which isn't yours or mine,

Because of our refusal to leave the blasphemy behind.

Hell's fires are burning brightly for the slanders defeat,

All of our sacrifice has been given to the idols and their deceit.

But with intervention in our self-seeking times,

With confession and repentance, salvation we still can fine.

Death is the penalty for the sin we demonstrate,

But God forgives and gives grace and mercy for us to appreciate.

Jeremiah 5:31,
    The prophets prophecy falsely, and the priests rule by their own power; and my people love to have it so. But what will you do in the end?

The Reason

Turn about, turn about, come
out of that prison,
You know the place the
courts send us when we
commit treason.
God gave the orders, no
defiance was needed,
But the bad seed was planted
in the garden of Eden.
Satan's energy was full of wrath,
And the time is coming for
his very last laugh.
Possessed with jealousy,
that is his reason,
The time has come to give
love on demand,
It's the one thing we have in
the palm of our hands.
With confidence that through
Jesus we're no longer
deceived,

Because life in the garden

is what we'll retrieve.

Romans 13:1,

Everyone must submit himself to the governing authorities, for there is no authority except that which God has established. The authority that exist have been established by God.

Standing on Holy Ground

I heard the sermon just a few weeks ago,

And I sat in that parking lot and let my anger grow.

As soon as I said it, it meant I had lied,

When I told Jesus I could swallow my foolish pride.

God said, Jesus was the answer to all of my stress,

But right at that moment, I knew I was possessed.

It's really so easy to lose all control,

You see Satan is waiting; he's big, bad, and bold.

And I was left feeling like I was totally blind.

But then I remembered I had to confess,

And that through Jesus alone would I come out of this blessed.

Proverbs 19:11,

The discretion of a man makes him slow to anger, and his glory is to overlook a transgression.

Nine Eleven's Measure of Faith

We watched from home
that awful day,
As human lives were wipe away.
No one knew the reason why,
But on this day we all would cry.
Some things we do are often bad,
And sometimes they
make others mad.
When we fail to let the Spirit thrive,
Knowing Jesus is always by our side,
Remember our savior has
already passed the test,
And how we should do nothing less.
Now it's time to take a stand,
By walking in the Master's plan.
It shouldn't have taken such
drastic measures,
T know God's Word must
be our treasure.

2 Peter 3:10,
But the day of the Lord will come like thief. The heavens will disappear with a roar; the elements will be destroyed by fire, and the earth and everything in it will be laid bare.

Suicide

When life seems to have

left me behind,

And all of my love ones

don't seem to mind.

My money's short I can't pay my bills,

So I have decided to swallow

all these pills.

I'm thinking about the easy way out,

Because right now I can't

see another route.

But all of a sudden, I stand to my feet,

I hear this sweet voice as

it begins to repeat.

Call Jesus! Call Jesus! He's

got you on his mind,

He'll remove all things that keep you confined.

He knows that you're lonely

in need of a friend,

Because only through Jesus

will your misery end.

Proverbs 8:35,
    For whoever finds me finds life, and obtain favor from the Lord;

Stop Crying and Fight Back

There is a fight unlike no other,
The fight to keep our salvation
alive and encourage
our brother.
Encouragement of self lets
the blessings flow,
Keeping Jesus in our hearts
will strengthen us so the
blessings continue to grow.
Tell yourself daily that faith
is the substance of
things hoped for,
The evidence of those things
that have changed
because of the Lord.
Then begin to fight the good fight of faith,
Because Jesus is coming back
soon, and there's no
time to waste.
Now stop your crying and
fight the enemy back,
You've got to tell that mean
and evil devil you've
had enough of his crap.

Galatians 4:6-12,

And because you are sons, God has sent forth the Spirit of His Son into your hearts, crying out, "Abba, Father!" Therefore you are no longer a slave but a son, and if a son, then an heir of God through Christ.

But then, indeed, when you did not know God, you served those which by nature are not gods. But now after you have known God, or rather are known by God, how is it that you turn again to the weak and beggarly elements, to which you desire again to be in bondage? You observe days and months and seasons and years. I am afraid for you, lest I have labored for you in vain.

Brethren, I urge you to become like me, for I became like you. You have not injured me at all.

Wait till the Harvest

Satan is still sowing seeds

of distraction,

He doesn't seem to care

that there will be

repercussions.

But the righteous man is still

growing before the

harvest takes place,

He has planted his seeds of

faith, which will be seen

all over his face.

He knows of the hidden

treasures that will be

revealed to him,

And he'll never let the enemy

kill, steal, and destroy

them.

The message was to wait till

the harvest, all who

won't be the sons of the wicked one,

They are those who hear and

know where the Word

comes from.

But for the enemy the fires

will be burning at an at

alarming rate,

Because they didn't take the

time to seal their fate.

Matthew 13:30,

Let both grow together until the harvest, and at the time of the harvest I will say to the reapers, "First gather together the tares and bind them in bundles to burn them, but gather the wheat into my barn,"

The Vision

The vision is to bring family
back together again,
To keep watch over our house
and correct the error
within.
But for me to love family
sometimes depends on
what they can do for me,
To love my family unconditionally
is what brings forth unity.
God's Word says to love the
loveable and those who aren't.
I've heard those words many
times, but I choose to
just sit back and grunt.
I know the rules of my savior
were meant to
transform,
And I'd have to be receptive
so my mind no longer
roams.
Then I'll exemplify my actions
with the word of God,
Because nothing I do through

him is supposed to be

too hard.

I can imagine these facts as

they begin to take

control,

A curative remedy that heals

down to the soul.

Then never let old habits

keep drawing me back,

Because family is important,

it doesn't come with a

contract.

Proverbs 29:18,
   Where there is no vision, the people perish: but he that kept the law,
happy is he.

Whatever You Say Lord

Whatever you say Lord,

whatever you say,

I know that I'll trust you, I

know it's your way.

God gave you the power,

to bridle my tongue,

To never hurt others with

the things that I say,

My heart will be open, I've

learned how to pray.

I thank the Lord Jesus, I

thank him today,

All that I am after is to

love God your way.

Whatever you say,

I will obey Lord, and do what you say.

I know that I'll trust you, I

know it's your way,

Whatever you say Lord,

whatever you say.

Proverbs 1:7,
   The fear of the Lord is the beginning of knowledge, but fools despise wisdom and instruction.

Hope

As long as his love stays deep inside,

Jesus is why we'll always survive.

The way we live our lives

has got to be,

Staying in prayer, it's what

will keep us free.

And with the hope of so much more,

We'll know God will open every door.

His blessing for us is what we desire,

So the life we lead must be

what God requires.

As we humble ourselves before thee,

God's direction in life is

what others will see.

And we'll thank the Lord

for all he's done,

Showing us hope is truly

for everyone.

Romans 5:5,
Now hope does not disappoint because the love of God has been poured out in our hearts by the Holy Spirit who was given to us.

In Bible study, we talked about curse reversal, all the negativity that has been passed down through generations of believing change wasn't possible. Now this doesn't mean that every aspect of life is going to be easy, only that with a new outlook, trials and tribulations can be dealt with differently from what we saw in past situations. The hard times will still sometimes come, but if we remember that Jesus came to restore what was lost when sin took over, the hope of so much more comes into view. If I never live another day after I finish this, I'll know that someone reading this may take some sort of action in changing the enemies' curse in their lives.

There isn't a lot I want to say about myself, except that I had to learn how to remove me from whatever I was going through, and sometimes that hurt. I'm no perfect, and sometimes people will push you to your breaking point. Hard lessons are what give you strength. Fight hard to keep your self-respect, while you remember to respect others in the process. Mistakes will be made by us all, but love conquers all. My poetry is just the rhyming of words, but I couldn't have done it without the gift coming from God. Much love to all my family and to those who have given me hope through what they have taught me.

Hope

Our Father's Love

Our Father's love is better than anything we could ever think or say,

It's this love that teaches us your

word, your will, and how to love others in Jesus's way.

And never be worried that our hearts will be torn apart,

We can trust that he'll be with us right from the very start.

Teaching Jesus is the source of how

our lives should be defined,

Our Father's love is what we should never leave behind.

Love is where the world began and where it all will end in God's way.

Our Father loves us more than mere words could ever say.

God's love is what has brought forth changes in and to us,

And it makes us rethink the things that we think
we need, but in him we have to trust.

Our Father gave us Jesus, and like him, in us he has to be,

And gave thanks to the Lord who has made known

God's deeds that we can see.

1 John 4:7,
    Beloved, let us love one another, for love is of God; and everyone who loves is born of God and knows God.

Stop Scratching

Stop scratching before you scratch yourself to death,

Take some time to think, and please take a deep breath.

And there you go scratching before God even asks you a question.

He wants you to try to remember the suffering of Christ,

And that he never gave an answer he knew wasn't right.

But there you go scratching because you've
said something you can't take back,

All the time knowing what you said was not the facts.

Lurking around with those itching ears,

And those who don't know will only see things as they appear.

But God's doctrine wasn't meant that we would slip through the cracks,

By not hearing the spirit and believing his acts.

False teacher will be teaching, but we must persevere,

Letting them know that God's Word is what's always clear.

Proverbs 15:2,
   The tongue of the wise uses knowledge rightly, but the mouth of fools
pours forth foolishness.

Pass Me My Cup Lord

Pass me my cup, Lord, that I may complete God's will,

When my cup is empty, God's will is fulfilled.

If we don't drink from God's cup, where would we be?

Sinking deep in sin without eyes that see.

The Word say the spirit is willing, but the flesh is weak,

But only if we kill the flesh will God's blessings begin to peak.

Surrendering is what Jesus did, God's will to be done,

He knew that God's blessings were soon to come.

Jesus endured the sacrifice; he never thought to run,

After he would return to his Father, and they would continue to be one.

Matthew 26:42,

Again, a second time, He went away and prayed, saying O My Father, if this cup cannot pass away from me unless I drink it, Your will be done.

Fighting My Failures

How could I continue to put me first?

Only thoughts of what I needed became my daily curse.

Why didn't I know you were waiting for me to ask for help?

I finally believed you care, and my heart began to melt.

So I went to the word and started my search,

He said to be still and know that I know what goes on this earth.

You have to endure whatever pain you're in,
Life is a process, and on me you must depend.

Your failures doesn't mean it's over we must try again,

Because with Jesus all things are possible where there is no sin.

Psalm 105:4,
Seek the Lord and His strength; Seek His face evermore!

It's a Celebration

The scripture says, "Let us rejoice and be glad and give Him glory,"

Because in each of our seniors there is a story.

Today they celebrate and reminisce together,

Thankful always for the past years and how
they have only made their lives better.

This afternoon is devoted completely to God,

Because he said to take care of our seniors with
the love that comes from our hearts.

So they will eat turkey, mashed potatoes, greens, and yams,

Now their stomachs are full, and they can get on with fellowship plans

The true meaning of this day is about to begin.

Celebrating thanksgiving and sharing blessings with friends.

They'll sing old and new songs and praise our God,

The music they tap their feet to that gives them a charge.

And when the afternoon has come to an end,

They have rejoiced with the Lord and they'll say amen.

November 20, 2010

A New Beginning with Jesus

It was Jesus who told us he would go

To his Father's house and prepare for us a place,

Because he knew we would soon come together, face-to-face.

Close your eyes and imagine the wonder of it all,

As John describes the blessing, even the foundational wall,

Twelve is the number that is symbolic of God's call.

The twelve tribes of the children of Israel, and the twelve apostles too,

God, Jesus, and the angels are who God's
Word says will also be with you.

The glory of the Lord will bring it all into our sight,

We know that up in heaven, we'll never experience night.

Streets of gold and pearls are the gates, New
Jerusalem's pure joy, it's God's amazing grace.

No more heartache, no more pain,

There will never be a need for us to cry again.

Jesus has delivered us, and God's praise will never end.

New Jerusalem is the place where God's
family comes together without sin.

Revelations 21:9-18

Pressing

Pressing forward through the thick and the thin,

The high call of God gives me reason to sing.

Keeping straight the melody that comes into my head,

An attainable mark from all that I've read.

I've changed my way of thinking because it's what Jesus said,

Blessing, not cursing is my new daily bread.

But there were still some things that I didn't understand,

Then the Holy Spirit gave me direction and a different game plan.

He told me what I needed; it was all in God's word,

I had to learn how to use it; it couldn't just be what I'd heard.

I knew how to be humble, or so I thought,

But didn't know how to be rich in what Jesus had taught.

So I'm now pressing through the thick and the thin,

My strength comes from Jesus, and there is no better friend.

The book of Philippians, 8/19/11.

The Good Stuff

8/25/11

The good stuff that the lost son was going to receive
from his father only lasted a little while,

The Father back in that day gave his son his request,
but in today's world, that's not a parent's style.

To give a child his inheritance when they know you're still alive,

The fact that he even asked was because of selfish pride.

Impatient was his character, and he soon did get his way,

And wasted his inheritance on the games that he would play.

But Lord God almighty when he had to feed the swine,

His stomach was so empty, normal food he could not find.

He thought about the pig pen and how his life could end,

If he didn't repent at once and admit that he had sinned.

He would return home to his family, and begin his life amend,

Because the father knows it is a blessing the
good stuff is life without sins end.

Luke 15:14-32

The Weather

I asked myself, what am I supposed to see when I look at the clouds?

Is it what will be waiting above them for me if Jesus will allow?

The formation of God's glory that I might see what he wills me to see,

What I see as I look at their wonder, the change is how he answered me.

You're not the person that you were years ago,
letting your mind jump to and fro,

Sometimes like the weather, a little unstable
and back then you refused to grow.

God is the creator of each and everything,

And in the clouds he had formed was a message he had arranged.

So when we give praise, glory, and honor to God on a regular basis,

It's hard to miss what he is teaching if we're willing to embrace it.

Acts 17:24-25,

God, who made the world and everything in it, since He is Lord of Heaven and Earth, does not dwell in temples made with hands. Nor is worshiped with men's hands, as though He needed anything, since He gives to all life, breath, and all things.

Why

Why our tears sometimes a needed friend?

They are sometimes the help that we need to mend.

Even Jesus wept before giving his life to save our souls.

He knew his love for us was about to unfold.

If he'd let pride get in his way, we would not have seen the light,

So he went up on the mount of Olives and shed tears from our life.

He said, "My Father tour will to be done,"

Those words were going to teach us that Jesus was God's son.

And he'd never let what was going on, on the outside,
destroy the love he had on the inside,

His heart he would not hide.

So we keep on pressing forward into our righteousness through Christ,

Never letting anything stop us, hope brings it all into our sight.

Remember Jesus is our shepherd, and he expects
us to hear him when he talks,

He's always there with us if as Christians we do walk.

Matthew 26:42,
    Again, a second time, He went away and prayed, saying, "O my Father, if this cup cannot pass away from me unless I drink it, your will be done."

Live, Love, and Act Like Jesus

WWJD, these were the letters that were written on many of the souvenirs a few years ago. They were meant to make us give some thought to our actions as we loved, live, and acted like Jesus from day to day. In this world today, we have to start our day asking ourselves, what would Jesus do and what won't Jesus do?

Jesus won't ever tell us he loves us just to get something from us. He loves us and it doesn't matter if we give him love back or not; he won't stop loving us. Today we see all kinds of evil everywhere, and we have to keep what Jesus won't do in our thought process. Busy is what the enemy is, and he'll destroy every life in his path if we let him.

Jesus said that if we were without sin, we should be the first to let it be known, but because we know that all have sinned, God gave us his son to teach us a better way through the example of how Jesus loved, lived, and acted while here on earth. He showed us what he wouldn't do, and then he showed us what he would. One of our biggest faults is sitting in judgment of others, and that's something we are never to do.

Every day we see new signs of his return, and judgment day is getting a little closer. But are we watching and listening to that still small voice and living for that special time? There is another saying that we still say a lot -been there, done that- but the reality is only Jesus has. He pressed forward to find those who would believe in what he would not do, then he shared with them the right way. The way God's word was designed, especially for us because we were still lost trying to do things our way.

There are so many things we wouldn't do if Jesus was truly in us. He'd never stand around trading insults with his brother and get so mad that they would come to blows. Anger is a powerful emotion that has to be overcome with love. When learning something new for the first time, we practice it over and over until we master it. What I'm writing isn't something new in every aspect- remember Cain and Abel, the brothers of the Bible, who were an example of unresolved anger.

All of us have a desire to be first and the best at what we do, and we forget to love our brothers and sister as God's Word has told us to. Joseph's story is of a brother who wouldn't do anything to harm his brothers, and it didn't matter that they weren't so nice to him. What he went through turned out to be a blessing to others as well as to them. His brothers let their anger take complete control of them, but Joseph loved them the most when it counted.

There is so much jealousy that is a part of our nature, and it makes it hard to love, live, and act like Jesus, especially in our Christian walk. We have to remember that Jesus and the Father are one, and the only way we join them in heaven, is if we take stock of the way Jesus love, live, and acted from a heart of love.

My Testimony of God's Saving Grace

When the choir was singing, "Take me back to a place where I first received Him." I closed my eyes, and I was taken back to a childhood memory. I was on my knees praying, and I had fallen asleep in that position; at the time, I didn't really know Jesus and how loving him would change my life.

My mother was teaching me that God didn't like the ugly, bad things children do, and I know that at the time I didn't listen. But as the choir sang, I was taken back to the place where I really first received him, the place where I was baptized. It was March 26, 1996, I was forty-three years old. This time, I knew I needed Jesus in my life.

It's not easy to put yourself out there like I've done in this book, but I've gone through most of what you are reading, and I can say that I am still open to whatever Jesus wants to teach me next. Moving forward means that I have to have an open mind, but more importantly an open heart.

Going back doesn't mean I'm stuck in the past; it can help me see the progress that I've made that has blessed my future. So take me back, dear Lord, whenever necessary that I might hear from you.

Amazingly Amazing

I think about where I am right at this moment,

God is there with me, it's a part of his covenant.

Daytime, nighttime, he's right there, Heaven or hell, he's not unaware.

If I have wings of an angel, I know he supplies the air,

His hand is always leading; he really loves me, and this he shares.

He covered my mother before I came into this life,

Wonderfully magnificent I am, God made me just right.

Everything about me God put into place,

So I must praise him, for my God-given grace.

He lifts up my spirit and inspires me to stay in his sight,

Because all of his inspiration will one day take flight.

So I now look at myself from his point of view,

I've been born again through Jesus, and what you see is brand-new.

The Looking Glass

Behold! The looking glass in it I see, All of
my features God has given to me.

I've been made to express as I look the rest,

That God made me completely, I'm the best of his best.

There is no other that looks just like me,

He made me distinctively so I'd be who he sees.

Psalm139:14,
   I will praise you for I am fearfully and wonderfully made.

www.ingramcontent.com/pod-product-compliance
Lightning Source LLC
Chambersburg PA
CBHW031323060726

47590CB00003B/1318